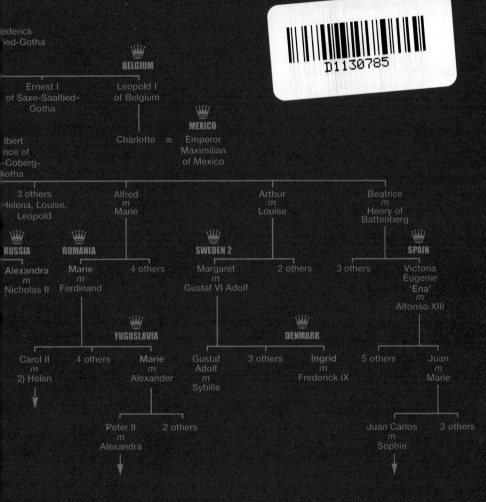

ederick
ied-Gotha

BELGIUM

Ernest I
of Saxe-Saalfied-
Gotha

Leopold I
of Belgium

MEXICO

lbert
nce of
-Coberg-
otha

Charlotte = Emperor
Maximilian
of Mexico

3 others
Helena, Louise,
Leopold

Alfred
m
Marie

Arthur
m
Louise

Beatrice
m
Henry of
Battenberg

RUSSIA

ROMANIA

SWEDEN 2

SPAIN

Alexandra
m
Nicholas II

Marie
m
Ferdinand

4 others

Margaret
m
Gustaf VI Adolf

2 others

3 others

Victoria
Eugenie
'Ena'
m
Alfonso XIII

YUGOSLAVIA

DENMARK

Carol II
m
2) Helen
↓

4 others

Marie
m
Alexander

Gustaf
Adolf
m
Sybille

3 others

Ingrid
m
Frederick IX

5 others

Juan
m
Marie

Peter II
m
Alexandra
↓

2 others

Juan Carlos
m
Sophie
↓

3 others

nealogical table showing how the British Royal Family became linked with other foreign ruling monarchies

Ex Libris

Margaret
McElfresh

We are very amused!

We are very amused!

From Mom,
Christmas 2006

ENGLISH HERITAGE

First published in Great Britain in 2005 by
English Heritage Kemble Drive Swindon SN2 2GZ

Packaged by Susanna Geoghegan
Text copyright © Michele Brown

ISBN 1850749485

Printed in Thailand by Imago Publishing

Introduction

While it is true that Queen Victoria probably uttered the legendary phrase 'We are not amused', it was not because she did not like fun and laughter. She was simply rebuking a courtier who had overstepped the bounds by telling a risqué story in the presence of a very young girl. Yet in many people's minds this one sentence has damned both Victoria, who loved to laugh, and the Victorian age, which was so diverse and dynamic, as dull and miserable.

Queen Victoria reigned for nearly sixty-four years, from 1837 to 1901 – longer than any other British monarch. To her subjects, both at home and abroad, she and her realm seemed almost indestructible.

We are very amused!

During her lifetime Britain dominated the globe and rapidly created the largest and most powerful empire the world had ever known. In far-flung places the Queen's name is still to be found: Victoria Falls and Lake Victoria in Africa; the Australian states of Victoria and Queensland; Hong Kong's Victoria Harbour, Victoria Peak and Victoria Road; and Mount Victoria in both Auckland and Wellington in New Zealand. So it is hardly surprising that her name has become synonymous with the nineteenth century wherever English is spoken and in many places where it is not!

But Victoria's longevity and the extent of British influence are not enough to account for the extraordinary resonance which her name and image still convey, over a hundred years after her death and more than a century and a half since she came to the throne as a young girl of nineteen. She also had a strong personality with clearly defined opinions and a sense of self which would have made her a formidable character in any walk of life. She did not merely reflect the spirit of her epoch; she also helped to shape it.

Above all Victoria had the great good fortune to have been Queen during one of the most significant and memorable eras ever recorded. The association with a period of extraordinary change and phenomenal progress

We are very **amused**!

(although change and progress are not always the same thing) has given her name a very special resonance.

During the nineteenth century science and technology saw the introduction of the railways, steam engines, electricity, telephones, sound recording, motor cars and aviation, to mention only a few of the many significant breakthroughs which, coming hard on the heels of the industrial revolution, altered the nature of the world for ever. Philosophers and thinkers such as Charles Darwin voiced theories that challenged the accepted teachings of the church, which had been the bedrock of western society for over a thousand years. The population expanded rapidly, turning Britain into a country of large industrial towns and cities where for centuries it had been an unchanging landscape of rural villages. Printing became easy and cheap, enabling the rapid spread of ideas and news to a population which would once have been in blissful ignorance of what was being done by its ruling elite. Trade expanded to make Britain the richest nation on earth. Yet this huge wealth was also a cause of friction where once people had been content to accept their station in life.

During such an unsettling time the Queen and her family came to represent stability and a set of consistent and reliable values which also became synonymous with the word Victorian. She and her husband, Prince Albert, were a loving couple and devoted parents, with a strong sense of duty. They created a model role for the royal family which became part of the unwritten British constitution and they set an example of fidelity and wholesome living which others have not always found easy to follow.

Osborne House, Isle of Wight

We are very amused!

Victoria and Albert's impeccable morals, combined with the stern, unbending image projected by the 'widow of Windsor' in her black mourning clothes during the long period she shut herself away following Prince Albert's early death, have also associated the word Victorian with the unattractive meanings of killjoy or hypocrite. Those who never knew the young woman were left with the impression that the Queen was fundamentally miserable and humourless. Nothing could be further from the truth. She was certainly not a killjoy – she loved what she called 'mirth'. Nor was she a hypocrite. In fact she was remarkably open-minded and tolerant and highly critical of those who took the high moral ground without exercising compassion.

For far from being dour and miserable Victoria was full of life and gaiety and came to the throne determined to enjoy herself after a heavily chaperoned childhood cut off from the company of other young people. She particularly loved music and dancing. As an unmarried woman etiquette forbade her to 'valse' because of the close contact between the partners. After she and Albert married the Queen made up for lost time, organising dances which lasted into the small hours and at which the amiable but less energetic Albert was often seen nodding off quietly in a corner.

We are very amused!

Queen Victoria found much else to amuse her, including romantic novels, falling in love, painting and drawing, good food, pretty clothes (her taste was sometimes a little questionable), the company of children, charades, Christmas festivities, picnics, a good malt whisky, visits to Paris, holidays on the Cote d'Azur, politics, her pet dogs, gossip, witty conversation and keeping an uninhibited and stylish journal packed with insights into her complex character and interests.

Victoria shouldered the enormous responsibilities of Queen and Empress and her name came to symbolise one of the most dynamic periods of British history. Her journal and letters, together with the memoirs of her contemporaries, paint a very different picture from the cliché of a narrow-minded woman living in tedious times. They reveal a complex, endearing and attractive woman with a keen sense of humour, who was endlessly curious about the exciting world around her and above all, in her own words, '*very much amused indeed*' by all it had to offer.

We are very amused!

Abraham's Bosom

Towards the end of her life the Queen was greatly saddened by the death of her much loved son-in-law, Prince Henry of Battenberg, who had been serving in South Africa. On a dismal February day on the Isle of Wight the Queen was sunk in thought and uncommunicative as she took her customary drive. Leila, Lady Errol, an old friend, tried to cheer her up:

'Oh, Your Majesty, think of when we shall see our dear ones again in heaven!'

The Queen was unforthcoming.

Her companion soldiered bravely on, 'We will all meet in Abraham's bosom.'

'I will *not* meet Abraham,' declared the Queen firmly.

(The Queen remarked later, in her journal, 'Dear Leila, not at all consolatory in moments of trouble!!')

Admirers

'I am sorry to say I have fallen hopelessly in love with the Queen, and wander up and down with vague and dismal thoughts of running away with a maid of honour.'

Charles Dickens, 1840

We are very amused!

'The three women I have admired most are Queen Victoria, Sarah Bernhardt and Lillie Langtry – I would have married any one of them with pleasure.'

Oscar Wilde, 1901

The eccentric Scottish poet, William McGonagall – 'Dundee's best remembered nobody' – was one of the Queen's most ardent admirers. He once walked all the way from Dundee to Balmoral in the pouring rain to see the Queen, only to be turned firmly away at the gates by an unfeeling servant.

Not even the Queen herself was safe from McGonagall's truly execrable verse, as this fragment from *An Ode to the Queen on Her Jubilee Day* demonstrates:

Therefore let all her subjects rejoice and sing,
Until they make the welkin ring;
And let young and old on this her Jubilee be glad,
And cry, 'Long Live our Queen!' and don't be sad.
And as this is her first Jubilee year,
And will be her last, I rather fear;
Therefore, sound drums and trumpets cheerfully,
Until the echoes are heard o'er land and sea.

We are very amused!

Albert

'Such beautiful blue eyes, an exquisite nose, & a pretty mouth with delicate moustachios & slight, but very slight whiskers: a beautiful figure, broad in the shoulders and fine waist.'

Queen Victoria, *Journal*, during Prince Albert's second visit to England

'*None* of you can *ever* be proud enough of being the *child* of SUCH a Father who has not his *equal* in this world – so great, so good, so faultless …'

Queen Victoria, letter to The Prince of Wales, 1857

'The Prince is become so identified with the Queen, that they are one person, and as He likes and She dislikes business, it is obvious that, while she has the title he is really discharging the functions of the Sovereign. He is King to all intents and purposes.'

Charles Greville, Diary

When in doubt about 'who's to blame', play Prince Albert, it is always a trump card, and ten to one it does the trick.

F. Airplay Esq., *Prince Albert – Why is he Unpopular?*

/ /

We are very amused!

In middle age Prince Albert became partially bald. In order to keep his head warm he took to wearing a wig at breakfast.

We are Amused

'It always entertains me to see the little things which amuse Her Majesty and the Prince, instead of their looking bored as people so often do in English Society.'

Lady Georgiana Bloomfield

'I have often heard my father speak of the Queen's intense amusement on one occasion when he was present and the Duchess of Atholl told the story of the comical advertisement regarding the Dunkeld and Blairgowrie coach, which was once posted in the village of Dunkeld. The coach was named "The Duchess of Atholl" and the inn from which it started was the "Duke's Arms". The notice ran as follows: "The Duchess of Atholl leaves the Duke's Arms every lawful morning at six o'clock."'

Patricia Lindsay, daughter of Colonel Robert Lindsay, equerry to the Prince of Wales

'I went with the Queen and the Prince last night to the Haymarket Theatre to see the *Beef and Orange*, a fairy tale plot, and awfully stupid, as Lady Canning and I agreed, but the Royal couple laughed very much and

We are very amused!

seemed to enjoy it of all things. It is certainly a nice thing about them that they are so easily amused.'

Eleanor Stanley, maid of honour

Angels

As the 81-year-old Queen lay dying at Osborne House her large extended family gathered around her, talking among themselves and sharing their memories of her amazing life. Knowing her strong views on everything – God and the Church had not been spared her robust opinions – someone brought up the subject of whether or not the Queen Empress could be happy in heaven.

'I don't know,' mused the Prince of Wales. 'She will have to walk behind the angels – and she certainly won't like that!'

Animals

'You'll be smothered with dogs.'

Lord Melbourne to Queen Victoria

Dash, Eos, Boy, Boz, Sharp, Noble, Lily, Maggie, Spot, Marco, Turi.

Names of Queen Victoria's favourite dogs

13

We are very amused!

Here lies
DASH
The favourite spaniel of Her Majesty Queen Victoria
In his 10th year
His attachment was without selfishness
His playfulness without malice
His fidelity without deceit
READER
If you would be beloved and die regretted
Profit by the example of
DASH

Memorial to Queen Victoria's first dog, 1840

'The one exception to the Queen's large-hearted sympathy with the animal kingdom is made with regard to cats. These the Sovereign holds in the greatest abhorrence, and not one of them is allowed to be where she is likely to see it.'

The Private Life of the Queen by One of Her Majesty's Servants, 1897

In 1887, while on holiday at Aix les Bains, Queen Victoria rescued a badly treated donkey, called Jacquot, from a French peasant. The Queen, who was finding it increasingly difficult to walk, took to travelling around in a small pony phaeton pulled by her little donkey. She could drive herself and remain independently mobile so this became her preferred method of private travel. It was less restful for her attendants, who were expected to keep up with the carriage while trotting alongside on foot.

Appearance

'A drawing room yesterday, at which Princess Victoria made her first appearance, a short vulgar looking child.'

Charles Greville, *Diary*

As a child, Queen Victoria had a sprig of holly pinned to the neck of her dress, to make sure she kept her chin up and did not slouch forward.

The Queen believed her eyebrows were too thin and had to be dissuaded by Lord Melbourne from shaving them to make them grow thicker.

'Qui est donc la reine?'

The puzzled citizens of Cherbourg. The Queen dressed so simply and unaffectedly they could not believe she actually was the ruler of the largest Empire in the world.

'The Queen stepped down wearing a large white hat with streamers floating behind, and marabou feathers on top. Her flounced dress was entirely

We are very amused!

white, and a bright green sunshade and mantle completed her costume. She wore small slippers tied with black ribands over the instep and ankle. A large bag or reticule, embroidered with a gilt poodle, hung from her arm. This was all *so different* from our Paris fashion.'

Empress Eugénie, the epitome of French chic, recalling Queen Victoria's startling outfit on her arrival in Paris, 1855

Art

'You have got to be careful of artists. You do not know where they have been.'

Queen Victoria

'The Queen's bosom has been most deliciously handled and has been brought out by the artist in full rotundity.'

Art critic's review of a portrait of Queen Victoria, *The Times*

16

We are very amused!

Assassination Attempts

Seven attempts were made on Victoria's life between 1840 and 1882. Her stoic attitude towards these attacks greatly strengthened her popularity.

In July 1842 a four-foot hunchback, Mr John William Bean, fired into the carriage carrying Victoria and Albert along Constitution Hill. Victoria and Albert appeared to have had a lucky escape. However the event was not quite as serious as it appeared at the time. Mr Bean had loaded his gun with tobacco and paper!

The last attempt on Queen Victoria's life was on 2 March 1882. Roderick McLean, who suffered, like all the Queen's potential assassins, from severe mental problems, fired at the Queen's carriage when she arrived at Windsor station. The Queen's unlikely rescuers were two Eton schoolboys, who intercepted the would-be assassin and beat him soundly around the head with their rolled-up umbrellas.

'It is worth being shot at to see how much one is loved.'

Queen Victoria, letter to her daughter Victoria, Crown Princess of Prussia, March 1882

We are very amused!

Babies

'Abstractedly I have no *tender* for them till they become a little human; an ugly baby is a very nasty object and the prettiest is frightful – till about four months; in short as long as they have their big body and little limbs and that terrible froglike action.'

Queen Victoria, letter to her daughter Victoria, Crown Princess of Prussia

'I don't dislike babies, though I think very young ones rather disgusting.'

Queen Victoria, letter to her daughter Victoria, Crown Princess of Prussia

'You know perfectly well that I do not hate babies (quite the contrary if they are pretty) but I do hate the inordinate worship of them and the more disgusting details of their animal existence, which I try to ignore.'

Queen Victoria, letter to her daughter Victoria, Crown Princess of Prussia

Birthdays

'After luncheon the children played.

Arthur and Alice a little duet.

Louise a little piece alone, fairly but not in time.

We are very amused!

Alice and Lenchen a duet beautifully.

Alice and Alfie on the violin a little composition of his own – very pretty and of which he is not a little proud.

Alice a long, beautiful and very difficult sonata by Beethoven. Arthur recited a German poem, and Lenchen and Louise have something to say – which however has not yet been said.'

Queen Victoria on her 39th birthday celebrations, in a letter to her eldest daughter, Victoria, Crown Princess of Prussia, 1858

Bishops

Throughout her life Victoria loathed bishops. As a child she had been terrified of them as they loomed over her in their strange wigs and aprons or worse still, got down on their venerable hands and knees to play with her.

As a very old woman her dislike remained as steely as ever. Attending a reception of bishops at Lambeth Palace for the 1897 Diamond Jubilee celebrations, she expressed her opinion forcefully to Lady Lytton:

'A very ugly party. I do not like bishops.'

'O, but your dear Majesty likes *some* bishops.'

'Yes, I like the man but *not* the bishop.'

We are very amused!

'Henceforth you must remember that Christ Himself will be your husband.'
Randall Davidson (later Archbishop of Canterbury) to Queen Victoria
after the death of Prince Albert in 1861

'That is what I would call twaddle. The man must have known that he was talking nonsense.'
Queen Victoria

Body Piercing

A completely uncorroborated rumour began to circulate during the nine-teenth century that the Prince Consort had resorted to a form of intimate body piercing in order to make his appearance more seemly in the tight, lightweight trousers which were fashionable at the time. There is no reputable evidence for this whatsoever. However the rumour persists to this day and at establishments where piercing of male genitalia is available the procedure is referred to as a 'Prince Albert'.

John Brown

John Brown was the Scottish gillie Queen Victoria came to rely on after the death of Prince Albert. She liked the way he treated her as a real woman rather than the Sovereign. He had a weakness for drink, was frequently over-familiar and caused a good deal of ill feeling within the family and the court but he was devoted to the Queen.

〜

'My beloved John would say: "You haven't a more devoted servant than Brown" – and oh! How I felt that!

Afterwards so often I told him no one loved him more than I did or had a better friend than me; and he answered "Nor you – than me. No one loves you more."'

Queen Victoria, talking after John Brown's death to his brother, Hugh, 1883

〜

The closeness between the Queen and John Brown led to scurrilous rumours that they were lovers and the Queen was referred to in the popular press as 'Mrs Brown'.

〜

Although John Brown was the favourite, his four brothers also worked for Queen Victoria. Donald Brown worked at Osborne House, Hugh Brown was Keeper of the Kennels at Windsor Castle, James Brown was the shepherd at Balmoral and Archibald Brown was a page in the royal household.

〜

While on a visit to her relatives in the German town of Coburg Queen Victoria was greeted by the German guard with the customary formal presentation of arms. Unfortunately, a programme of very loud military drumming, which showed no signs of coming to an end, followed this ceremony.

'Oh, I wish they would turn in,' protested the Queen, as the agonising din continued.

Undaunted, John Brown, who did not speak one word of German, sprang forward and silenced the astonished drummers with the authoritative command:

'Nix boom boom!!'

'Once in Scotland, after a picnic luncheon taken at Glassalt Shiel, the Queen asked for a table to be brought from the cottage at which she could sit and make some sketches. Table after table failed to suit the Queen's taste, and the servants were at their wits' end. Suddenly Brown awoke to the situation, picked up one of the discarded tables, planted it in front of the Queen and said:

"It'n na possible to mak' anither table for you up here."

The Queen admitted the common sense of Brown's remark and used the table.'

The Private Life of the Queen by One of Her Majesty's Servants, 1897

The Queen was well aware of John Brown's fondness for drink but tolerated it even when it incapacitated him. On one occasion, when he keeled over completely, she excused him to those present, by declaring that she herself had 'distinctly been aware of an earthquake shock'.

We are very amused!

'Balmoral. Tuesday. "Court Circular"
     Mr John Brown walked on the slopes.
     He subsequently partook of a haggis.
     In the evening Mr John Brown was pleased to listen to a bagpipe.
     Mr John Brown retired early.'

Satirical version of the Court Circular in *Punch* magazine

After Brown's death in 1883 a grieving Queen Victoria wanted to write her own biography of him, *The Life of John Brown*. She was dissuaded by her advisers, who thought the unique event of a Queen writing the biography of one of her servants would fuel the rumours of a romantic attachment between them.

After Brown's death in 1883 a grieving Queen Victoria wanted to write her own biography of him, *The Life of John Brown*. She was dissuaded by her advisers, who thought the unique event of a Queen writing the biography of one of her servants would fuel the rumours of a romantic attachment between them.

Although dissuaded from writing John Brown's life story, the Queen took the unprecedented step of dedicating her second published book, *More Leaves*, to him. She also insisted on including a paragraph about him in the text, at a time when it was unthinkable to refer to servants as equals.

Celebrity

It was said that Queen Victoria occasionally visited the central London home of Baroness Burdett-Coutts in order to watch, unseen, from an upper floor window, the hustle and bustle of Piccadilly going on below. When asked why this was so enjoyable she replied, 'Yours is the only place where I can go to see the traffic without stopping it.'

As newspapers became increasingly popular the Queen often found herself harassed by the presence of 'gentlemen of the press', who hung around outside her home waiting to follow her when she emerged.

This was a particular problem at Balmoral, where the reporters hoped to catch the Queen and her family off their guard enjoying their informal holiday pastimes. Although protocol meant that the reporters should stay out of sight the Queen caught sight of a carriage full of them, which proceeded to follow her as she went for a drive. The Queen promptly ordered her carriage to turn sharply about and retrace its route. The carriage full of reporters was forced into a ditch as the royal vehicle swept by and the Queen had the last laugh as she watched their discomfiture.

'The important thing is not what they think of me, but what I think of them.'

Queen Victoria, when told her subjects were complaining that she shut herself away from public view after Albert's death

The Queen was disconcerted to find that the arrival of two of her children on a visit to New York provoked the distinctly New World newspaper headline, 'VIC'S CHICKS'.

We are very amused!

Character

From an early age Victoria set great store by honesty and direct speaking. A tutor inquired of the Duchess of Kent whether her daughter had been a good little girl that day and the Duchess replied, 'Yes, she has been good this morning, but yesterday there was a little storm.' At which the four-year-old piped up, 'Two storms – one at dressing and one at washing.'

'Great events make me quiet and calm; it is only trifles that irritate my nerves.'
Queen Victoria

Princess Marie-Louise, Victoria's granddaughter, relates a personal experience of the Queen's uncompromising honesty. At the age of one the little Princess had been left with her brothers and sister in the care of their grandmother, while their parents holidayed in the south of France. The Queen sent the absent parents a reassuring telegram:

'Children very well but poor little Louise very ugly.'

Years later Princess Marie-Louise asked her grandmother what had made her send such an unkind telegram.

Back came the no-nonsense reply:

'My dear child, it was only the truth!'

We are very amused!

'It is in one's own power to be happy – and to be contented.'

Queen Victoria

Childbirth

'One has a strong wish to give a husband a good, strong ducking ... what humiliations to the delicate feelings of a poor woman, especially with those nasty doctors.'

Queen Victoria, *Journal*

'What you say of the pride of giving life to an immortal soul is very fine, dear, but I own I cannot enter into that; I think much more of our being like a cow or a dog at such moments.'

Queen Victoria, letter to her daughter Victoria, Crown Princess of Prussia

Childhood

Victoria was breastfed by her mother, the Duchess of Kent, who believed firmly in the benefits of 'maternal nutriment'. This was highly unusual in an era when most aristocratic babies were farmed out to a wet nurse.

We are very amused!

Victoria's upbringing was completely dominated by her ambitious, widowed mother: the Princess was required to sleep in her mother's room and was prohibited from speaking with anyone unless her mother or her German governess was present.

When William IV died and Victoria inherited the throne the Duchess of Kent visited Victoria immediately the formalities were over to ask if there was anything she could do for her daughter. Exercising her new independence the young Queen declared firmly, 'I wish to be left alone.'

Children

'It is indeed a pity that you find no consolation in the company of your children. The root of the trouble lies in the mistaken notion that the function of a mother is to be always correcting, scolding, ordering them about and organising their activities. It is not possible to be on happy, friendly terms with people you have just been scolding.'

Prince Albert, letter to Queen Victoria, October 1856

'They are in terror of the Queen.'

Sir Arthur Ponsonby, Private Secretary, on the Queen's relationship with her children

That Blessed Chloroform

The idea of pain relief for women in childbirth was strongly contested by nineteenth-century doctors and clerics, who were, of course, all men. Many actually believed it was necessary for women to suffer.

In 1853, boldly defying medical and religious convention, Victoria gladly accepted chloroform to ease the pain during the birth of her fifth child, Prince Leopold. In doing so she became a pioneer in the development of modern anaesthetics. Her doctor Sir James Clark wrote later:

'The Queen had chloroform exhibited to her during her last confinement … It was not at any time given so strongly as to render the Queen insensible, and an ounce of chloroform was scarcely consumed during the whole time. Her Majesty was greatly pleased with the effect, and she certainly never has had a better recovery.'

Victoria called the anaesthetic 'that blessed Chloroform … the effect was soothing, quieting and delightful beyond measure.'

Christening

Victoria's christening was a stressful occasion. Tsar Alexander I had consented to be a godfather and Alexandrina was therefore proposed as one of the baby's names in his honour. The Prince Regent, later George IV, had also (reluctantly) consented to stand as godfather to his niece. The eager parents thought they would flatter him by choosing Georgiana as the baby's principal name but this was firmly vetoed. The Prince was a stickler for formality, so the Tsar's name must take precedence over that of a Prince. But since the Prince Regent was not prepared to see his name take second place to anyone's, Georgiana had to be vetoed. So too were Charlotte (how dare they choose the name of his dead daughter) and Augusta (far too grand for such a poor relation).

As the Archbishop of Canterbury stood poised by the font, babe in arms, waiting to hear if a second name might be allowed, the Regent barked, 'Let her be called after her mother.' And so, at the last minute, the baby became Princess Alexandrina Victoria.

At the christening of Prince Albert Edward, the Queen's first-born son and therefore heir to the throne, the Dean of Windsor, somewhat tactlessly, congratulated the Queen on producing a boy and 'saving us from the incredible curse of a female succession'.

We are very amused!

Christmas

Queen Victoria's Hanoverian ancestors introduced the German style of celebrating Christmas to Britain in the eighteenth century but it was popularised by Prince Albert. In 1840 he set up a Christmas tree at Windsor for the first Christmas of his eldest child, the Princess Royal. Twenty years later a courtier described the royal family's Christmas:

'The Queen's private sitting rooms were lighted up with Christmas trees hung from the ceiling ... These trees, of immense size, besides others on the tables, were covered with bonbons and coloured wax lights ... These rooms contained all the presents for the royal family ... Lords, grooms, Queen and princes laughed and talked, forgot to bow, and freely turned their backs on one another. Little princesses ... in the happiest manner, showed each person they could lay hands on the treasures they had received ... I never saw more real happiness than the scene of the mother and all her children.'

'This morning we had a very pretty and brilliant amusement. The Queen took the Princess Royal, with me to hold her, in the sledge, the Prince driving. The sledge is quite pretty; beautiful grey ponies all covered with bells and sparkling harness; the gentlemen attending, and the scarlet grooms preceding and following, over the dazzling snow, in purest sunshine.'

Lady Lyttelton, Governess to the Queen's children

We are very amused!

Church Services

The Queen disliked High Church ceremony and preferred simple services conducted at a brisk, no-nonsense pace. For the 1887 Golden Jubilee she had many discussions with the Archbishop of Canterbury about the thanksgiving service to be held at St Paul's Cathedral. Far from relishing the prospect the Queen was determined to gallop through it as fast as possible. To every suggestion from the Archbishop her first response was 'Can this be shorter?' As a result the Queen was in and out of the cathedral in a very satisfactory thirty minutes. This was a source of considerable pleasure to Her Majesty but a serious disappointment to the Archbishop and to the Queen's loyal subjects.

'Too long.'

Queen Victoria's opinion of the Thanksgiving Service at St Paul's
for the recovery of the Prince of Wales from typhoid fever, 1872

'May she skip like a he-goat upon the mountains!'

This unexpected conclusion to a heart-felt prayer for his Sovereign, was offered up by the dour Minister at Crathie church. The Queen found it impossible to keep a straight face and her granddaughter, Princess Alice, later wrote, 'It was noticed afterwards how Grandmama was deeply moved by the prayer and buried her face in her hands.'

We are very amused!

Collapse of Stout Party

'While going over the castle with the Queen my mother brought her to her new boudoir, then in the course of being finished. My mother's kinswoman, old Lady Mexborough, was with us, and the Queen, who knew she was even older than she looked, said to her very kindly: "Please sit down."

Lady Mexborough thereupon sat down in one of the new and incomplete chairs that had not been seated and her partial disappearance was very swift and dramatic. Queen Victoria's strict sense of decorum was not quite proof against the incident.'

Earl of Warwick, *Memories of Sixty Years*

Coincidence

Victoria was named after her German mother. Fortunately Victoria was also almost exactly the name of Admiral Nelson's flagship, *The Victory*. This made the name unexpectedly popular with patriotic Britons who were known to dislike anything that sounded foreign.

We are very amused!

The Common Touch

A fellow Balmoral gillie was chatting to John Brown as he prepared to accompany the Queen back to Buckingham Palace.

'Ye must see a lot o' grand folks in London, John?'

'Me and the Queen pays nae attention to them,' was the down-to-earth reply.

~

'The Queen is a homely little thing *when she is at her ease*, and she is evidently dying to be always more so.'

Thomas Creevey, *Diary*

Conversation

Victoria was bilingual and spoke only German up until the age of three. She and Albert generally spoke to each other in German. The Queen also spoke French and Italian and a smattering of Hindustani, as well as being competent in Latin.

Although her English was completely fluent, speaking German influenced the Queen even in her old age. This occasionally resulted in strange turns of speech. On one occasion when her Prime Minister, Lord Salisbury, reported that the Kaiser was stirring up trouble in

Europe she earnestly entreated him to 'do all you can to pour oil on the flames'.

Small talk at formal occasions was not the young Queen Victoria's strong point as Charles Greville made clear when, in his diary, he recorded for posterity this particularly painful example of a conversation going in ever-decreasing circles.

Queen: 'Have you been riding today, Mr Greville?'

Greville: 'No, madam, I have not.'

Queen: 'It was a fine day.'

Greville: 'Yes, ma'am, a very fine day.'

Queen: 'It was rather cold though.'

Greville: 'It *was* rather cold, madam.'

Queen: 'Your sister, Lady Francis Egerton, rides I think, does not she?'

Greville: 'She does ride sometimes, madam.' (A pause when I took the lead though adhering to the same topic.)

Greville: 'Has your Majesty been riding today?'

Queen: (With animation): 'O, yes, a very long ride.'

Greville: 'Has your Majesty got a nice horse?'

Queen: 'O, a very nice horse.'

It was a similar experience, many years later and with another monarch, which prompted Joyce Grenfell's mother to remark, 'When royalty leaves the room it is like getting a seed out of your tooth.'

We are very amused!

'I can hardly tell you all the things she talked about. Prince Humbert – Garibaldi – Lucy (Lady Lyttelton) – the Hagley boys – smoking – dress – fashion – Prince Alfred – P of Wales's visit to Denmark – revenue – Lancashire – foreign policy – the newspaper press – the habits of the present generation – young men – young married ladies – clubs – Clarendon's journey – the Prince Consort on dress and fashion – P of Wales on ditto – R Meade – Sir R Peel – F Peel – misreading foreign names and words – repute of English people abroad – happy absence of Foreign Office disputes and quarrels.'

Prime Minister William Gladstone, to a friend, describing dinner with Queen Victoria at Windsor

'H.M. don't like being bored.'

Sir Henry Ponsonby, Private Secretary to the Queen

Dancing

As a young woman Victoria loved dancing – from Scottish reels to Georgian minuets. At a ball given for her during her second State Visit to France in 1855, she was paid the delicate compliment of having 'God Save the Queen' played as a polka.

We are very amused!

'I am agreeable to see that your Queen dances like a pot.'

Prince John of Glucksburg, Danish courtier. (He had, of course, meant to say she dances like a top!)

'After supper they danced a Mazurka for ? an hour ... the Grand-Duke, asked me to take a turn, which I did, (never having done it before) and which is very pleasant ... After this we danced (which I had never seen before) the 'Grossvater' or 'Rerraut', which is excessively amusing. I danced with the Grand-Duke, and we had much fun and laughter ... It begins with a solemn walk round the room; which also follows each figure; one figure, in which a lady and gentleman run holding their pocket-handkerchief by each end, and letting the ladies on one side of it go under it, and the gentlemen jump over it, is too funny ... I never enjoyed myself more. We were all so merry.'

Queen Victoria, *Journal*, 1837

'It is quite a pleasure to look at Albert when he gallops and valses, he does it so beautifully, holds himself so well with that beautiful figure of his.'

Queen Victoria, *Journal*, during Prince Albert's second visit to England

Discretion

When Prince Albert became Chancellor of Cambridge University in 1847 he and Queen Victoria paid a visit to be shown around the delights of the

We are very amused!

city and its famous colleges. William Whewell, Master of Trinity College, together with a number of other important university figures, was charged with leading a royal sight-seeing party.

At that period the river Cam was still used as an open sewer. As the party paused on a bridge Her Majesty drew attention to the assorted flotsam and jetsam being carried downstream and to the remarkable number of pieces of paper clogging up the water. Pre-empting her next question the quick-thinking academic explained, 'All that paper, Ma'am, carries notices to inform visitors that the river is unfit for bathing.'

'A little rose in the front dear child, because of the footmen.'

Queen Victoria's gentle hint to her granddaughter, Princess Alice, when she wore a low-cut ball gown

Dolls

As a child collecting and dressing dolls was Victoria's favourite hobby. She was highly skilled with her needle and with the help of Baroness Lehzen she created scenes from history or her favourite operas with wooden dolls – 132 in total – for which she designed and made the costumes herself.

We are very amused!

Earliest Memories

Asked by her granddaughter, Princess Marie-Louise of Schleswig-Holstein, what were her earliest memories the old Queen replied, 'Going to Carlton House Terrace to watch Sir Thomas Lawrence paint the Duchess of Gloucester.'

Empress of India

In 1876 Queen Victoria was given the additional title of Empress of India. This ensured that the Sovereign of the world's largest empire at last had a title to match her exalted position and did not have to defer to Imperial Russia and Germany.

The man who brought this question to a satisfactory conclusion was her Prime Minister, Disraeli. A few months later Disraeli himself was elevated to become Lord Beaconsfield prompting the satirical magazine *Punch* to observe drily 'one good turn deserves another'.

We are very amused!

A Family Affair

The First World War broke out thirteen years after Victoria's death. It was called 'a family affair' because so many of the European monarchies, including those of Russia, Germany and Austria-Hungary were related through Queen Victoria. This made life painful for the members of this extended, but previously close-knit family, who were fighting on opposite sides.

In addition to being at war with Great Britain, ruled by his cousin George V, Victoria's grandson, Kaiser Wilhelm II of Germany, also invaded Russia, a country ruled by Tsar Nicholas II, nephew of Victoria's daughter-in-law, Queen Alexandra, and husband of Queen Victoria's granddaughter, Princess Alix of Hesse.

Tsar Nicholas II probably spoke the truth when he wryly observed:

'Had she been alive at the start of the conflict Victoria would never have permitted it.'

Firsts

As a child Victoria became the first member of the royal family to be vaccinated against smallpox.

We are very amused!

In 1843 Queen Victoria made a State Visit to England's old enemy, France, where she met the liberal monarch Louis-Philippe at the Chateau d'Eu near Dieppe. This was the first State Visit by a ruling British monarch since 1431.

The custom of holding garden parties at Buckingham Palace was begun in Queen Victoria's reign, when they were called breakfast parties.

Queen Victoria instituted the Victoria Cross in 1854. The first person to receive the medal from the Queen, at the first investiture on 26 June 1857, was Commander Henry Raby.

Food

'People should only eat when they are hungry.'

Prime Minister Lord Melbourne to Queen Victoria.

'In that case I should be eating all day.'

Queen Victoria's reply.

When she was a child, little Victoria was often chastised by her mother for the bad habit of 'gobbling' her food. Despite this, as an adult she still always ate very fast. Court etiquette required everyone to stop eating and the footmen to clear the plates immediately the Queen had finished her own food, so Victoria unwittingly caused a lot of unhappiness by this bad habit.

On one occasion Lord Hartington was heard boldly to call out, 'Here, bring that back,' when a 'scarlet marauder' whisked away a half finished plate of mutton and peas from under his nose.

A lady-in-waiting was asked to bring her small daughter to luncheon with the Queen – a great honour but stressful for the mother when there was so much etiquette, not to mention the unpredictable behaviour of a young child, to contend with.

The little girl was carefully coached by her nanny beforehand: no speaking with a full mouth, no chewing with the mouth open, no fidgeting, no speaking unless spoken to, no eating with fingers etc. etc. As the luncheon progressed, and her daughter behaved immaculately, the mother began to relax. At that point fresh asparagus was brought in and the little girl watched horrified as the Queen herself picked up an asparagus spear with her fingers. As the Queen took a bite the child could not contain herself any longer. She leaped from her seat and raced round the table. Wagging her finger at Queen Victoria she scolded her soundly, saying, 'Piggy, piggy,' in a perfect imitation of her nanny.

We are very amused!

One of the daily duties of a maid of honour included placing a bouquet on the right hand side of the Queen's plate on the dining table.

While staying at her villa in the French Riviera, the Queen and her ladies paid a visit to a zoo belonging to the Comtesse de la Grange, a woman of uncertain origins. The Comtesse made Victoria a gift of an ostrich egg. Before presenting it to the Queen the Comtesse had scrawled her signature on the egg. 'Just as if she had laid it herself,' observed the Queen mischievously to her lady-in-waiting.

However the Queen had to admit that the omelette which her chef later made from the egg was 'delicious'.

As she grew older the Queen's digestive system began to suffer under the strain of years of over-eating. Her physician recommended substituting rich food with a bland diet of Benger's invalid food and chicken. Unfortunately the Queen liked the Benger's so much she began taking it in addition to her usual menu.

'A list of the dainties sent to Her Majesty at Balmoral on September 1st, 1892, may be interesting to those who share their Sovereign's weakness of a "sweet tooth".

     1 Box of Biscuits
     1 Box Drop Tablets

We are very amused!

- 1 Box of Pralines
- 16 Chocolate Sponges
- 12 Plain Sponges
- 16 Fondant Biscuits
- 1 Box of Wafers, containing 2 or 3 dozen Fancy Shapes
- 1? dozen Flat Finger Biscuits
- 1 Sponge Cake
- 1 Princess Cake
- 1 Rice Cake

This order, which with sundry varieties is expected three or four times a week, is always addressed thus:

"This package to be delivered at the Equerries' Entrance at Buckingham Palace."

From thence the Queen's Messenger conveys it to the Court'

The Private Life of the Queen by One of Her Majesty's Servants, 1897

In later years the Queen's favourite food was ice-cream. Marie Mallet, a lady-in-waiting, wrote in her diary that the 81-year-old Queen could not really expect to avoid the trials of indigestion when 'she devours a huge chocolate ice, followed by a couple of apricots, washed down with iced water'.

We are very amused!

Funerals

The Duke of Kent, Queen Victoria's father, was so stout that at his funeral the over-sized coffin became jammed in the doorway to the family vault at Windsor.

Despite years of wearing black in mourning for Prince Albert, Queen Victoria surprisingly stipulated that her funeral trappings should be white and that cream horses should pull the gun carriage at a full military funeral.

The horses waiting in the cold at Windsor Station to pull the gun carriage with Queen Victoria's coffin on the last stage of its long journey from Osborne to St George's Chapel at Windsor Castle, grew restless and uncontrollable. A quick-thinking officer swiftly unharnessed the horses and substituted 'bluejackets' – naval ratings from the Naval Guard of Honour. This unplanned incident, which resulted in the heavy gun carriage being pulled by her loyal sailors, became the most moving and memorable image of the Queen's funeral and a new tradition was born.

We are very amused!

Garter Ceremony

'The Queen fumbled ostensibly, as she always does, to show her unfamiliarity with the slightly indiscreet article of male attire.'

Lord Clarendon, observing the Queen's clumsiness while fastening the Order of the Garter to the leg of Napoleon III

Gifts

On their tenth birthdays Queen Victoria gave each of her grandchildren a solid gold watch.

The Queen gave Prince Albert a silver lunch box to keep his sandwiches fresh while he was out all day stalking deer in the Scottish Highlands.

The funeral car of Napoleon I was presented by Queen Victoria to the French nation. The gift was formally delivered to Prince Napoleon at Les Invalides in Paris, where Napoleon I lies buried.

We are very **amused!**

'Her presents to those about her invariably consist of jewellery or pieces of silk or lace, while at one time Her Majesty was very fond of going round her gardens and conservatories and herself selecting the flowers she wished to wear in the evening.'

The Private Life of the Queen by One of Her Majesty's Servants, 1897

Grandmother of Europe

'I delight in the idea of being a grandmamma; to be that at 39 … and to look and feel young is great fun, only I wish I could go through it for you, dear, and save you all the annoyance. But that can't be helped. I think of my next birthday being spent with my children and grandchild. It will be a treat.'

Queen Victoria, letter to her daughter Victoria, Crown Princess of Prussia, 1858

'I fear the seventh grand-daughter and fourteenth grandchild becomes a very uninteresting thing – for it seems to me we go on like the rabbits in Windsor Park!'

Queen Victoria, letter to her daughter Victoria, Crown Princess of Prussia, 1868 after the birth of the Prince of Wales's new daughter, also Princess Victoria

We are very amused!

The Great Exhibition

Prince Albert was responsible for the hugely successful Great Exhibition of 1851, which his proud wife attended on more than forty occasions. On one of these visits she was attracted by the stand of an American soap manufacturer. This stand was decorated with wonderful statues and carvings made of soap. They looked so perfect that the Queen believed they were really made of marble. She was just about to test one by scratching it with her shawl pin when the owner leant forward to prevent her. The Queen graciously excused this breach of protocol after the loyal American explained: 'Pardon, Your Majesty, but you see, it *is* the head of *Washington.*'

'The tremendous cheering, the joy expressed in every face, the vastness of the building, with all its decorations and exhibits, the sounds of the organ, and my beloved husband the creator of this great "Peace Festival", uniting the industry and art of all nations of the earth was quite overwhelming.'

Queen Victoria, *Journal,* June 1851, on the opening of The Great Exhibition

Grog

'The Queen and Prince Albert were relaxing on deck during the Channel crossing to France for their State Visit in 1843, when the Queen was asked to move to a different deck chair.

Asked why, the Captain explained:

"The fact is, Your Majesty is unwittingly closing the door of the place where the grog tubs are kept, and so the men cannot have their grog."

"Oh, very well," said the Queen, "I will move on one condition, viz., that you bring me a glass of grog."

This was accordingly done, and after tasting it the Queen said, "I am afraid I can only make the same remark I did once before, that I think it would be very good if it were stronger."'

Georgiana, Lady Bloomfield, *Reminiscences*, 1883

The Highlands

'Scotch air, Scotch people, Scotch hills, Scotch rivers, Scotch woods, are all far preferable to those of any other nation, in or out of this world …'

Queen Victoria, talking to Lady Lyttelton

We are very amused!

Holidays

As a child Victoria was taken on what she called 'holly days' to Ramsgate and Broadstairs. These were popular resorts at the time because the bracing sea air of the North Kent coast was believed to be good for the health.

It is often assumed that once Balmoral and Osborne House were built, Queen Victoria took all her holidays either in Scotland or the Isle of Wight. In fact Queen Victoria was a trendsetter who travelled extensively throughout Europe. In 1882, aged 62, she visited the French Riviera for the first time and fell in love with the area she called 'a paradise of nature'. She visited the area nine times, staying at Cimiez near Cannes or in Nice.

Because of the Queen's patronage the French Riviera became a popular holiday destination for the crowned heads of Europe and wealthy Americans, which made Victoria very popular with her French neighbours.

John Brown regularly accompanied the Queen when she holidayed on the Riviera but he did not enjoy the experience. Never one to adjust to local customs, he insisted on wearing his kilt, despite the hot weather, and in addition sported a solar topee to keep off the sun; this sartorial combination, not surprisingly, caused a great deal of comment among the local population.

The train on which Victoria made the journey to the south of France had a special royal saloon, with convertible sofa beds and a dining car. This was attached at Calais or Cherbourg where the Queen arrived after crossing the Channel. An important element of the royal baggage was a copper kettle so that the Queen could enjoy a good British cup of tea while on foreign soil.

'Oh, if only I were at Nice, I should recover!'

Queen Victoria, during her last illness, 1901

Early in their marriage Victoria and Albert visited the magnificent Italian city of Florence. Prince Albert, who loved architecture (he was responsible for designing Balmoral and Osborne), was fascinated by the architectural treasures of the city. The magnificent dome of the cathedral, which had been built by the renaissance genius Brunelleschi, particularly over-whelmed the Prince and Victoria.

Some years after Albert's premature death the Queen visited Florence again and was taken to see the cathedral, where the dome had been newly restored and was looking even more magnificent. A touching moment was observed as the Queen stopped her carriage in the piazza outside the cathedral. The window was pulled down and the Queen opened her locket, in which she kept a picture of Prince Albert, and held the picture out towards the dome so that he could share the special moment with her. After a few silent minutes with her memories, she closed the locket, the window was rolled up and the carriage drove away.

Homes and Palaces

'Tartanitis.'

An anonymous opinion of Prince Albert's Scottish themed décor at Balmoral

⌐⌐⌐

'They would rejoice the heart of a donkey, if they happened to *look like* his favourite repast, which they don't.'

Lord Clarendon's disparaging remark about the ubiquitous thistles used as a decorative motif at Balmoral

⌐⌐⌐

Beech logs were always burned in the fireplaces of the private apartments of all her residences as the Queen had a strong dislike of coal.

⌐⌐⌐

'Her Majesty's conservatism in the arrangement of her own apartments is very touching, particularly when viewed by the light shed by the small

We are very amused!

cards affixed to the doors of all her rooms in her various residences, which say that everything within was chosen and arranged by her late husband, the Prince Consort, and has to all intents and purposes remained unaltered since his death.'

The Private Life of the Queen by One of Her Majesty's Servants, 1897

Honours

On a visit to St Leonard's on the south coast Princess Victoria's carriage overturned. The two horses, which were entangled in the wreckage, became dangerous as they lashed out in their panic to break free. One eventually escaped and galloped away, completely out of control and a danger to itself, the passengers and passers by. Three years later a Mr Peckham Micklethwaite, who had courageously brought the terrified beast to a halt by sitting on its head, was created a Baronet in Queen Victoria's Coronation Honours.

Housewifery

'Only in knitting was Her Majesty ever awkward, and she acknowledges herself, with a hearty laugh, the justice of a remark made by an old peasant woman, who, unaware of the Queen's personality, picked

We are very amused!

up a scrap of knitting that Her Majesty had done, and curtly observed that she pitied her "gude mon" if he got no better made stockings than that.'

The Private Life of the Queen by One of Her Majesty's Servants, 1897

Insults

'Nowadays a parlour maid as ignorant as Queen Victoria was when she came to the throne would be classed as mentally defective.'

George Bernard Shaw, Irish writer

'General Sir Lyndoch Gardiner, one of the Queen's Equerries, was one of (John) Brown's pet aversions, although he was quite unconscious of the fact ... On one occasion he came into waiting and on meeting Brown he enquired how the Queen was and what she had been doing lately. Brown replied, "The Queen's very well. It was only the other day she said to me, 'There's that dommed old fool General Gardiner coming into waiting and I know he'll be putting his bloody nose into everything that doesn't concern him.'"

History does not relate what General Gardiner replied.'

Fritz Ponsonby, son of the Queen's Private Secretary

We are very amused!

journal

Victoria's German governess, Baroness Lehzen, was the person who taught her to keep a journal. From the age of thirteen therefore, Victoria recorded the events of just about every day of her life. As a result we know more about the intimate thoughts and events of Queen Victoria's life than of any British monarch before or since.

Lehzen herself wisely chose not to keep a journal in case it fell into the wrong hands.

Kind Heart

'Once the Duke of Wellington brought her a death warrant to sign, the soldier being an incorrigible deserter. The Queen evinced extreme reluctance to affix her signature, and pressed the Duke for some reason for clemency. At length the Duke admitted that the condemned man had always earned the affection of his fellow soldiers. The Queen, with tears in her eyes, cried, "Oh, Your Grace, I am so pleased to hear that," and hastily wrote "Pardoned, Victoria R." across the slip of paper.'

The Private Life of the Queen by One of Her Majesty's Servants, 1897

We are very amused!

When Victoria's granddaughter, Princess Helena Victoria of Schleswig-Holstein, was holidaying at Balmoral, she asked her grandmother if she might have a game of tennis with two of the maids of honour (fraternising with servants, even maids of honour, was not generally encouraged). Queen Victoria agreed, but only 'so long as you pick up the balls yourself. Being Sunday, I do not think it right to make others work for your amusement.'

Literature

Queen Victoria wrote to Lewis Carroll to say how much she had enjoyed his hugely popular children's book, *Alice in Wonderland,* and letting him know that she would very much like to read some of his other works. Lewis Carroll was the pen name of Charles Dodgson, a mathematics don at Oxford. A few weeks later the Queen was disconcerted to receive a copy of the author's latest, and somewhat less entertaining, publication entitled *Syllabus of Plane Algebraical Geometry.*

Two extracts from the Queen's journal, illustrated with her own water-colours and drawings, were published in her lifetime. The first, *Leaves from the Journal of Our Life in the Highlands*, was published in 1868 and became a best seller, with sales of 20,000 of the first edition alone. In 1883 the Queen followed this with a second volume, *More Leaves from the Journal of A Life in the Highlands*.

We are very amused!

The Queen's family and court were disgusted by the unseemly prominence these books gave to servants.

'The trait that seems to be most prominent in Her Majesty's book is the tea tray.'

Review of *Leaves from the Journal of Our Life in the Highlands* in *Punch* magazine

John Brown's Legs or Leaves from a Journal in the Lowlands. (Dedicated to those extraordinary Legs, poor, bruised and scratched darlings ...)

Title of an American parody of Queen Victoria's best selling books, published in 1864

'From the humblest of writers to one of the greatest.'

Queen Victoria's inscription in the copy of *Leaves from the Journal of Our Life in the Highlands*, which she presented to Charles Dickens in 1870

The Queen and her high-minded daughter, the Empress Frederick of Prussia, were discussing the merits of Marie Corelli, whose novel *The Sorrows of Satan* was the runaway success of the 1890s. The Queen considered Corelli one of the greatest writers of the age. The Empress thought her a second-rate writer who would quickly be forgotten.

Fritz Ponsonby, who had not been listening to the discussion, was called over to give his unbiased opinion. Blissfully unaware of the danger,

We are very amused!

he declared that the secret of Corelli's popularity was her appeal to the semi-educated.

Unsurprisingly the Empress swiftly changed the subject.

'A strange, horrible business but I suppose good enough for Shakespeare's day.'

Queen Victoria after seeing *King Lear*

Longevity

'I don't mind praying to the Eternal Father, but I must be the only man in the country afflicted with an eternal mother.'

The Prince of Wales (later Edward VII) during the celebrations for Queen Victoria's Diamond Jubilee, 1897

Love and Marriage

'He clasped me in his arms and kissed me again and again.'

Queen Victoria, *Journal*, 1839, after her engagement

'Do you remember how I warmed your dear little hands every day in the lovely little blue room? In quiet hours I live on such memories. Good, dear charming Victoria, in my thoughts I am very much with you.'

Prince Albert to Queen Victoria, letter written shortly after their engagement, 1839

Victoria and Albert were very physically attracted to each other and enjoyed a lively love life. Their wedding on February 10th 1840 was followed by a honeymoon of three *'very very happy days'* at Windsor Castle.

'When day dawned (for we did not sleep much) and I beheld that beautiful angelic face by my side, it was more than I can express! He does look so beautiful in his shirt only, with his beautiful throat seen.

We got up at ? 8. When I had laced I went to dearest Albert's room, and we breakfasted together. He had a black velvet jacket on, without any neckcloth on, and looked more beautiful than it is possible for me to say …'

Queen Victoria, *Journal*, 11 February 1840

'My dearest Albert put on my stockings for me. I went in and saw him shave; a great delight for me …'

Queen Victoria, *Journal*, 13 February 1840

'A most gratifying and bewildering night.'

Queen Victoria to Lord Melbourne, recalling her wedding night, 1840

We are very amused!

'Oh, Sir James, am I to have no more fun in bed?'

> Queen Victoria to her obstetrician, Sir James Clark, when he
> suggested she should avoid having more children

Shortly after their marriage Queen Victoria and Prince Albert had a tempestuous quarrel. The Prince stormed out of the room and locked himself in his private apartments. Victoria followed, hammering furiously upon his door.

'Who's there?' Albert called. 'The Queen of England, and she demands to be admitted.' No response.

Victoria hammered at the door again. 'Who's there?' 'The Queen of England.' Still there was no response.

Victoria, with growing fury, hammered again and again to no avail.

At last there was a pause, followed by a gentle tap on the door. 'Who's there?' Albert asked. 'Your wife, Albert,' the Queen replied, and was promptly admitted.

'A marriage is no amusement but a solemn act & generally a sad one.'

> Queen Victoria, 1879, letter to her daughter Victoria, Crown Princess of Prussia

'Thy dear image I bear within me, and what miniature can come up to that? No need to place one on my table to *remind* me of *you*.'

> Prince Albert, explaining to Victoria why he had not taken her picture with him on a visit abroad

We are very amused!

'A well-known prejudice of the Queen is the one she entertains against the re-marriage of widows. On this point Her Majesty is quite immoveable ...'

The Private Life of the Queen by One of Her Majesty's Servants, 1897

Medical Matters

It is rumoured that Queen Victoria took cannabis tincture for her menstrual pains. Her personal physician, Sir Russell Reynolds, wrote in *The Lancet*, 'Cannabis, when pure and administered carefully, is one of the of the most valuable medicines we possess.'

In her sixties the Queen developed rheumatism. A French masseuse, Madame Charlotte Nautet, was employed to help alleviate the pain. Madame Nautet became known about Court as 'The Rubber'.

The Queen's son Prince Leopold lived at home even as an adult. He had inherited haemophilia and was often forced to rest for the sake of his health. On the day his first child was born Victoria had badly sprained her leg. Determined nonetheless to visit the new parents and baby as soon as possible the Queen had herself carried along the corridors to their apartment. As she later recalled:

'He was lying on the sofa, she on another and when I came as a 3rd helpless creature, it had quite a ludicrous effect.'

We are very amused!

Military Affairs

'You never saw anyone so entirely taken up with military affairs as she is.'

Lord Panmure, writing to Lord Raglan, 1855

After the defeat of the British troops at Colenso during the Boer War the Queen asked one of her granddaughters to instruct her Private Secretary, Sir Arthur Bigge, to 'clear the line' as she wished to telegraph the troops.

Sir Arthur sent a message back politely explaining that it was customary for the Sovereign to telegraph the troops only if they won a victory.

'And since when have I not been proud of my troops whether in success or defeat? Clear the line,' retorted Her Majesty.

The line was cleared and the telegram sent.

Victoria regularly reviewed her troops – although being in the presence of hundreds of fighting men in an era of poor personal hygiene could be challenging.

At one such review, accompanied by her Prime Minister, Lord Palmerston, she was driven to hold her handkerchief to her nose and mouth, beginning tentatively, 'There seems to be rather a …'

At which point Palmerston smoothly interrupted, 'Oh, that's what we call *esprit de corps*, Ma'am.'

We are very amused!

In 1900, Queen Victoria sent New Year's greetings to the troops stationed in South Africa during the Boer War, in the form of a specially moulded chocolate bar.

Mistaken Identity

A rather stout lady came down to a dinner party in Coburg wearing a white dress. Unfortunately one of the other guests, a very short-sighted gentleman, mistook the large white object in front of him for a wood burning stove, turned his back to her, parted his coat tails and proceeded to 'warm' himself by the fire.

A favourite after-dinner anecdote told by Prince Albert

Queen Victoria loved to tell the story of how one night, as she was leaning from her window at Windsor Castle, one of the sentries on duty had started to whisper sweet nothings to her because 'he mistook me for a housemaid!'

Queen Victoria loved to tell the story of how one night, as she was leaning from her window at Windsor Castle, one of the sentries on duty had started to whisper sweet nothings to her because 'he mistook me for a housemaid!'

For his birthday in 1857 Queen Victoria gave Prince Albert a charming gilded silver statuette of a stark naked Lady Godiva riding sidesaddle on her horse. George V, Queen Victoria's grandson, was particularly fond of the statuette. Fritz Ponsonby asked the King why this was. George V explained that he always remembered with pleasure the memorable

We are very amused!

occasion on which Queen Olga, the famously short-sighted grandmother of Prince Philip, Duke of Edinburgh, squinted down at the statuette and murmured approvingly, 'Ah, dear Queen Victoria.'

Misunderstanding

On one memorable occasion Queen Victoria was sitting next to elderly Admiral Foley at lunch. The Admiral, who was hard of hearing, was talking boomingly and in great detail of the operation he had supervised to salvage the frigate HMS *Eurydice*, which had sunk off Portsmouth.

Taking advantage of a momentary pause, the Queen attempted to change the subject by inquiring after the health of her friend, the Admiral's sister.

The Admiral, thinking he had heard a concerned inquiry after the state of his beloved ship, continued blithely and in the same loud voice:

'Well, Ma'am, I am going to have her turned over, take a good look at her bottom and have it well scraped.'

At this, the Queen was overcome by uncontrollable laughter and had to put down her knife and fork and hide her face in her handkerchief as the tears poured down her face.

We are very amused!

Morality

'The cold heartless world – or the very severe and religious ones – will not understand – though God will!'

Queen Victoria, 1870, to her daughter the Crown Princess of Prussia, on the elopement of a mutual acquaintance who was 'living in sin'

'Lady Blandford came by, I having allowed poor, divorced ladies, who have had to divorce their husbands owing to cruelty or misbehaviour, but are in no way to blame themselves, to appear at Court.'

Queen Victoria, 1887

The Queen was always interested in and concerned about the lives of her poorer subjects and eagerly quizzed a visiting churchman from the deprived East End of London on the conditions of the local people. He explained that things were so dire he had, on more than one occasion, known of people sleeping seven to a bed.

'Had I been one of them I should have slept on the floor,' commented the Queen firmly.

We are very amused!

Motor Cars

'I hope you will never allow one of those horrible machines to be used in my stables. I am told they smell exceedingly nasty, and are very shaky and disagreeable conveyances altogether.'

Queen Victoria to The Master of the Horse

Neglect

Towards the end of the Queen's life at Osborne her staff seemed to sense she was no longer a force to be reckoned with as these two observations by Marie Mallet, her lady-in-waiting illustrate.

'The Queen only ordered one small dish – nouilles – for her dinner last night and it was entirely forgotten, so she had nothing.'

'The footmen smell of whisky and are never prompt to answer the bell and although they do not speak rudely, they stare in such a supercilious way.'

Nicknames

As a child Queen Victoria was not know as Victoria but Drina, a diminutive of her first name, Alexandrina.

We are very amused!

One of Victoria's 'wicked uncles', the Duke of Gloucester, was known to the rest of the family as Silly Billy.

❧

The Prince of Wales (Bertie) earned the nickname Tum-Tum because of his huge appetite and later, because of his ever-expanding paunch.

❧

Victoria and Albert's first child, Victoria, the Princess Royal, was called Pussy or Pussette by her doting parents.

❧

Princess Alice, Victoria and Albert's second daughter, was known in the family as Fat Alice or Fatima.

❧

The Faery Queen or The Faery

Benjamin Disraeli's private names for Queen Victoria

❧

'The terrible old G man'

Queen Victoria's private name for Gladstone

❧

'Gangan'

The name given to her by Victoria's great-grandchildren

We are very amused!

Nudity

Both Victoria and Albert had a keen appreciation of male beauty and both drew the nude male figure. However Victoria did not draw from life models but only from photographs.

Paris

'I am delighted, enchanted, amused and interested, and think I never saw anything more beautiful or gay than Paris.'

Queen Victoria, 1855

The Emperor of France and his lady so gay,
Are coming to England – get out of the way,
There'll be baked frogs, and fried frogs, and frogs in a stew,
And all the young ladies shall sing *parlez-vous*.

Popular ballad at the time of the exchange of State Visits between Britain and France, 1855

We are very amused!

Photography

Queen Victoria and the art of photography were both born early in the nineteenth century and the Queen loved to record her life, family and possessions by 'fixing the picture'. She kept her own private photographer, Mr Cleave, and at Windsor Castle a dedicated photographic studio and developing rooms were created.

The Queen's family were among the first to be captured on moving film. The Queen later noted in her journal:

'We were all photographed by Downey by the new cinematograph process, which makes moving pictures by winding off a reel of film.'

Politics

'I am sick of all this horrid business – of politics and Europe in general, and think you will hear some day of my going with the children to live in Australia, and to think of Europe as of the moon.'

Queen Victoria, letter to her daughter Victoria, Crown Princess of Prussia

We are very amused!

'I love peace and quiet, I hate politics and turmoil. We women are not made for governing, and if we are good women, we must dislike these masculine occupations. There are times which force one to take interest in them, and I do, of course intensely.'

Queen Victoria, letter to her daughter Victoria, Crown Princess of Prussia

'That was a woman! One could do business with her.'

Prince Otto von Bismarck of Prussia, emerging from an interview with Queen Victoria, Berlin, 1888

Praise

Her court was pure; her life serene;
God gave her peace; her land reposed;
A thousand claims to reverence closed
In her as Mother, Wife and Queen.

Alfred, Lord Tennyson, *To The Queen*

'She's more of a man than I expected.'

Henry James, American writer

We are very amused!

Prime Ministers

The rivalry between Disraeli and Gladstone, both of whom served as Prime Minister, was legendary. The difference between them is charmingly encapsulated in the supposed remark of a young lady who had sat next to each of them at dinner. Asked for her impressions of the great men she summed them up:

'When I left the dining room after sitting next to Mr Gladstone I thought he was the cleverest man in England. But after sitting next to Mr Disraeli I thought I was the cleverest woman in England!'

Queen Victoria had much the same opinion.

'Fear God. Honour the King. Obey Your Parents. Brush Your Teeth.'

Lord Melbourne's four precepts for a successful life

'I never deny; I never contradict; I sometimes forget …'

Benjamin Disraeli on his strategy for handling the Queen

'Everyone likes flattery; and when you come to Royalty you should lay it on with a trowel.'

Benjamin Disraeli

We are very amused!

'He is full of poetry, romance and chivalry.'

Queen Victoria on Disraeli, letter to her daughter Victoria, Crown Princess of Prussia, 1868

❧

'We authors, ma'am ...'

Benjamin Disraeli's flattering greeting to Queen Victoria, following the successful publication of part of her journal under the title *Leaves from the Journal of Our Life in the Highlands*

❧

'Gladstone treats the Queen like a public department, I treat her like a woman.'

Benjamin Disraeli, on his rival William Ewart Gladstone

❧

'He speaks to me as if I was a public meeting.'

Queen Victoria, speaking of Gladstone

❧

'I love the Queen – perhaps the only person left to me in this world that I do love ...'

Benjamin Disraeli

❧

'The thought of composing it (the parliamentary tribute to Disraeli after his death) brought on diarrhoea.'

William Gladstone on his rival, 1881

We are very amused!

'The symbol of this vast Empire is a Crown, not a bonnet.'

Lord Rosebery, attempting to coax the Queen out of her mourning clothes

Protocol

In the nineteenth century it was still customary for the Home Secretary and other ministers to be present in the room during the birth of a potential future monarch, to ensure there had been no underhand substitution.

Understandably this was a matter of some embarrassment to the men who had to stay close to the royal bed during labour. Sir James Graham who witnessed the birth of Queen Victoria's son and heir, Prince Albert Edward, in 1841, was further embarrassed by being wrong-footed on a matter of protocol. Having cursorily inspected the new baby he offered the Queen his loyal congratulations 'on the birth of a very fine son'.

'A very fine *prince*, Sir James,' was her tart response.

In later years coming face-to-face with the legendary Queen Victoria could unnerve even the most sophisticated individuals.

At one investiture a high-ranking politician was due to be knighted by Her Majesty. Hovering at the door to the State Room, where the Queen was waiting with her ceremonial sword, he was heard to mutter nervously to the presiding official, 'What am I to do?'

'Kneel, kneel,' hissed the courtier.

We are very amused!

When the doors opened the man did not walk to the dais but fell immediately to his knees and waddled the length of the room towards the Queen 'like the funny man at a child's tea party'.

The Queen was unable to stop laughing at such a peculiar sight, particularly as, when she retreated, 'the little man followed' – still on his knees.

❧

In the company of her immediate family and her household the Queen much preferred to be addressed as 'Ma'am' rather than the formal 'Your Majesty'.

❧

'I have now been 30 years in harness and therefore ought to know what should be – but I am *terribly shy* and nervous and *always was so*.'

Queen Victoria, 1867

Reign

Queen Victoria reigned for 63 years and 216 days – longer than any other British monarch.

Relatives

Queen Victoria's grandfather was George III, who became ill and insane. Among the delusions of his illness was that he could have conversations with the trees in Windsor Great Park. Victoria was scarcely a year old when he died and she was not amused when asked by her granddaughter Princess Marie-Louise, if she had ever known the King.

'What, show a baby to a man who was mentally deranged? What an idea!'

As an old lady the Queen took to reminiscing about incidents in her youth and recalled seeing a statue of George III, but could not recall seeing an inscription. On being informed that the statue was actually inscribed in Latin, 'To the best of Fathers', by his son George IV, the Queen laughed aloud and exclaimed, 'The best of Fathers indeed! Why, they never spoke!'

The Duke of Kent, Victoria's father, was almost completely bald, prompting the playwright Sheridan to mock him with the observation that 'Grass doesn't grow on deserts.' The Duke proved he was not quite as dull as Sheridan believed by coming up with the response:

'If Sheridan means that I haven't genius I can tell him that such a gift would have been of small value to a Prince, whose business it is to keep quiet. I am luckier in having, like my country, a sound constitution.'

In the event the Duke had the last laugh for by the close of the nineteenth century his descendants ruled virtually every country in Europe.

As a very young child Victoria heartily disliked her uncle the Duke of Sussex. He lived next door and she was told he would punish her if she was naughty and made any noise. 'For which reason, I always screamed when I saw him!' she recalled nearly fifty years later.

Another of Victoria's uncles, the future King Leopold I of Belgium, had an eccentric taste in dress, which included wearing platform soles and a feather boa.

Queen Victoria's daughter-in-law, Alexandra, who was married to the Prince of Wales, suffered from deafness caused by her pregnancies. Keeping her involved in the conversation became a struggle, particularly for Victoria who was old and frail.

'The Queen was decidedly better this morning after a good night but a large luncheon party and shouting to the Princess of Wales exhausted her and she was in pain and very feeble after it.'

Marie Mallet, lady-in-waiting, letter, 1900

We are very amused!

One of the many distinguished guests who came to London in 1887 to celebrate Queen Victoria's Golden Jubilee was Princess Liliuokalani, who later became the last Queen of Hawaii. The two women got along famously but Queen Victoria was astonished when Princess Liliuokalani confided, 'Your Majesty, you may not be aware that I am a blood relative of yours.' Greatly intrigued the Queen asked how that could possibly be. 'My grandfather ate your Captain Cook,' was the cheerful, if unexpected, reply.

Reprimands

When Victoria wanted to reprimand a member of her extended family, even one living with her, she did not speak to the culprit directly but wrote a little note of reproof and sent it to them in a box labelled 'The Queen'.

The German Kaiser, Wilhelm II, was Queen Victoria's eldest grandchild. Unfortunately, during his reign the relationship between Great Britain and Germany deteriorated. When diplomatic relations were at a particularly low ebb the Emperor asked his cousin, Princess Marie-Louise, to write to their grandmother and suggest she make a detour to meet him and his ministers in Berlin on her way back to England from a holiday in Italy. The Queen's reply was to the point:

'Tell William that I appreciate his wish to see me. However, in my opinion it would be more fitting if the grandson were to travel to see his aged grandmother than that she should undertake a long and tiring journey to visit him.'

The Kaiser took the hint and made the journey himself.

The Irish Sea is notorious for being a difficult and squally crossing. On one visit to Ireland the Queen's ship was badly buffeted by the rough seas. Being fanatical about fresh air the Queen refused to go below deck for her own safety. Suddenly a particularly large wave came over the side and the Queen was almost swept away. When she had recovered she called one of her attendants to her, and issued the following instruction, 'Go up to the bridge, give the Admiral my compliments, and tell him that must not be allowed to happen again.'

'The Queen is very particular as to any form of dirt or even untidiness, and there is a story told of Her Majesty coming across a neglected cabinet in one of the little suites off the Grand Corridor, and writing her well-known signature with her finger in the dust. Going the next day to see the result of this silent rebuke, she found that no notice had been taken of it, and accordingly wrote the name of the particular housemaid who was responsible for the neglect underneath. The next day the two signatures had disappeared, and so had the housemaid ...'

The Private Life of the Queen by One of Her Majesty's Servants, 1897

We are very amused!

'The country, and all of *us*, would like to see you a little more stationary.'
Queen Victoria, attempting to curb the excesses of her playboy son, the Prince of Wales

'I remember Lord Melbourne using the same arguments many years ago, but it was not true then and it is not true now.'
Queen Victoria to Henry Campbell-Bannerman, who recalled feeling like a little boy being reprimanded by his grandmother

Republicanism

'A horse leech.'
The opinion of the anti-monarchy publication *Reynold's News* on the subject of Queen Victoria, 1871

The Queen's Resolve

When she was eleven Victoria's governess, Baroness Lehzen, drew her attention to the fact that she would probably inherit the crown. It was the first time the princess had fully realised the significance of her position. Her response was to say to Lehzen, 'I will be good.'

We are very amused!

With time the simple words of a child, which probably referred to the fact that she would try harder at her lessons, were vested with an almost holy significance and the statement became known as 'The Queen's Resolve'.

Respect

'Your Majesty may perhaps have heard that Ibrahim Pasha learned to write his name while your Majesty's messenger was waiting for the Queen's album; and that when he had written his name in the book he threw away the pen, saying that as the first time in his life that he had written his name had been for the Queen of England, so it should be the last, for he would never write it again for anyone else.'

Lord Palmerston, reporting on the Egyptian ruler's response to a request for his signature

Rings and things

'She wore geranium flowers placed here, there and everywhere. She had plump hands with rings on every finger, and even on her thumbs; one of these contained a ruby of prodigious size and of a superb blood red. She found it difficult to use her knife and fork with her hands thus laden with these reliquaries, and even more difficult to take off and put on her gloves.'

General Canrobert, reporting on the Queen's State Visit to France, 1855

We are very amused!

Servants

'All domestic servants who have any occasion to enter the Queen's presence have the strictest possible orders on no account to look at Her Majesty. Any servant found infringing this rule is severely reprimanded.'

The Private Life of the Queen by One of Her Majesty's Servants, 1897

Setting an Example

Queen Victoria and Prince Albert prided themselves on their virtuous family life and on setting an example to others. In the words of a 'royal' writer of the time, the Rev. Charles Bullock, 'The Queen's household has been – what every palace should be – a model home.'

The royal couple's success in putting this message across can be judged by the opinion of a Victorian theatregoer who had been shocked and outraged by Cleopatra's amoral antics in Shakespeare's *Antony and Cleopatra*, and who declared loudly on leaving the theatre,

'How different, how very different from the home life of our own dear Queen!'

We are very amused!

'We must all have our trials and vexations; but if one's *home is happy*, then the rest is comparatively nothing ...'

Queen Victoria, December 1841

Slapstick

One of the elements which first attracted Victoria to Albert was his liking for slapstick and juvenile practical jokes – a taste inherited by later generations.

'He went into immoderate fits of laughter at anything like a practical joke; for instance, if anyone caught his foot in a mat or nearly fell into the fire ... the mirth of the whole Royal Family, headed by the Prince, knew no bounds.'

Lady Mary Ponsonby, *A Memoir*

'We left Dalkeith on Monday, and lunched at Dupplin, Lord Kinnoul's, a very pretty place with quite a new house, and which poor Lord Kinnoul displayed so well as to fall head over heels down a steep bank, and was proceeding down another, if Albert had not caught him; I did not see it, but Albert and I nearly died laughing at the relation.'

Queen Victoria, *Journal*, 1842, on her first visit to Scotland

'Why bother to tell your best stories in a house where you get far louder laughter by shutting your thumb in the door?'

Lord Granville, despairing at the lack of sophistication at Court

We are very amused!

Smile

'No smile was the least like it, and no shadow of it preserved under the evil spell of the photographic camera … It came very suddenly, in the form of a mild radiance over the whole face, a softening and a raising of the lines of the lips, a flash of kindly light beaming from the eyes … Her smile, in fact, was the key to the secrets of the Queen's character.'

Mary Ponsonby, lady-in-waiting

'She was wreathed in smiles and, as she tattled, glided about the room like a bird.'

Benjamin Disraeli, 1874, describing an audience with the Queen

'So awe-inspiring was the first impression that I should have been terrified but for the wonderful, blue, child-like eyes, and the sweetest most entrancing smile I have ever seen on a human face.'

Dame Ethel Smythe

Smoking

Victoria did not approve of smoking, and regarded it as particularly reprehensible in women. However, while on picnics at Balmoral during the notorious midge season which plagues Scotland in the summer, her granddaughters were allowed to smoke cigarettes to avoid being bitten by insects. The Queen even tried a few puffs herself – but was not impressed, declaring the taste 'horrible'.

As Victoria's sons grew up they resented not being allowed to smoke with their friends. Victoria banned all smoking and even had *'No Smoking'* notices put up in her palaces. Like adolescents the world over the sons sought to outwit their mother by smoking in places they thought she would not visit. When she announced that there was to be an inspection to check on whether the rules were being obeyed they put up a sign – WC – on the door of their smoking room to deter their mother and all snooping womenfolk from coming in to make an inspection.

Snoozing

In her later years Queen Victoria was inclined to nod off, particularly at the dinner table or during one of her carriage drives. For her ladies-in-waiting keeping the Queen awake on occasions when she might be in the public eye became a major preoccupation. Marie Mallet, who was in waiting during the 1890s, wrote to her husband 'My evening task is now no light one, the Queen sleeps soundly and yet adjures me to keep her awake, even shake her if necessary, this I cannot bring myself to do, so I read and rustle the paper and wriggle on my chair and drop my fan and do all in my power to rouse my Sovereign, but she would be so much better off in bed and so should I.'

Spy

Last Monday night, all in a fright,
Al out of bed did tumble.
The German lad was raving mad.
How he did groan and grumble!
He cried to Vic, 'I've cut my stick:
To St Petersburg go right slap.'
When Vic, 'tis said, jumped out of bed,
And whopped him with her night-cap.

Anonymous ballad,1853. Prince Albert was rumoured to be a Russian spy
as Britain geared up for war against Russia in the Crimea.

Style

'Did you not observe how the Empress looked round to see if there was a chair for her before she sat down. But *your* Queen, a born Queen, sat

84

We are very amused!

down without looking. She knew a chair *must* be there, as surely as she is Queen of England.'

Comment during the Queen's State Visit to the Emperor Napoleon and Empress Eugenie, 1855

Supernatural

The possibility of being able to contact the dead was a consolation to Victoria after the death of her beloved Albert, and she was known to attend regular séances and to consult mediums.

This became such an obsession that when Benjamin Disraeli, her former Prime Minister, lay dying in 1881 he declined the offer of a consolatory death bed visit from his Sovereign, muttering anxiously,

'No, it is better not. She would only ask me to take a message to Albert.'

On the anniversary of Queen Victoria's death, her children would visit the mausoleum at Frogmore. One year, as they knelt piously in prayer, a dove entered the mausoleum and flew about.

'It is dear Mama's spirit,' they murmured.

'No, I am sure it is not,' contradicted Princess Louise.

'It must be dear Mama's spirit,' they persisted.

'No, it isn't,' said Princess Louise. 'Dear Mama's spirit would never have ruined Beatrice's hat.'

Thrift

Having been married to the frugal Albert and being the child of impoverished parents (all things are relative of course) Queen Victoria was inclined to be careful with her money, despite ruling the richest empire the world had ever known.

The story goes that one of her grandsons tried to persuade her to advance him £5 – a large sum at the time. She wrote back refusing to help him and admonishing him to learn the value of money. The young man took her advice to heart and promptly sold her letter for the princely sum of – £5!

Trains

Prince Albert was fascinated by technology and eager to show how the Crown was ready to embrace new inventions. At his request the Great Western Railway built an ornate state carriage for the Queen with a symbolic crown on the roof. On the inside the carriage was constructed like a small drawing room. On 14 June 1842, the Queen and Prince made their first train journey in it, travelling the line from Slough, near Windsor, to Paddington Station in London. Victoria announced herself 'quite charmed', but Albert worried that the locomotive's speed was dangerously excessive – an amazing fifty miles an hour.

We are very amused!

To ensure the comfort of the royal family the railway companies provided luxurious waiting rooms for them at the stations they used regularly, such as Windsor and Paddington. At Paddington the Great Western Railway also constructed a private room on the first floor, with a bowed glass window which overlooked platform one, so that Queen Victoria could sit and enjoy the novelty of watching the trains arriving and departing.

The London and North Western Railway constructed special saloons – one for day travel and one for night travel – to take the royal family to Scotland. To muffle any irritating noise from the wheels on the tracks the royal train had cork sound insulation sandwiched between a double floor. A felt underlay, on which was placed a thick carpet, then covered the floor.

Queen Victoria loved fresh air and cold temperatures – much to the discomfort of her retinue and family who were seated in howling draughts by open windows or made to accompany her on drives and walks in icy cold weather. To avoid being confined during the heat of the day the Queen made a habit of travelling overnight by train, when the air was coolest.

We are very amused!

Underwear

There is always intense interest when items of Queen Victoria's underwear come up for sale at auction. Although the Queen was very careful in her housekeeping it was rumoured that she wore new linen every day. This would mean that during a reign of 64 years she would have got through over 23,000 pairs of drawers.

〜

'It is a very vulgar error to believe, as many people do, that the "cast linen" given away by the Queen is body linen.'

The Private Life of the Queen by One of Her Majesty's Servants, 1897

Voice

Queen Victoria was the first member of the royal family to have her voice recorded after Edison patented the phonograph in 1878. When the cumbersome recording equipment was initially demonstrated to her she was unimpressed. But during a border dispute with Abyssinia in the last decade of the century she was persuaded by her advisers to send King Menelik of Abyssinia a personal phonographic message expressing her 'desire for friendship between our two Empires'. Although the Queen agreed to the recording she insisted that the wax cylinder be destroyed after he had heard the message. The message had the desired effect. Indeed, on hearing the Queen's disembodied voice, King Menelik solemnly rose to his feet as a token of respect. Following the resolution of the dispute the official envoy, Colonel Harrington reported, 'The cylinder was returned to me and immediately broken into pieces as promised.' Yet mysteriously a copy of it survived. It remains our only record of Queen Victoria's voice.

〜

'The Queen's voice is like a silver stream flowing over golden stones.'

Ellen Terry

〜

'Queen Victoria had a beautiful voice and first rate delivery at an age when she could not have played any part on the stage presentably except the nurse in Romeo and Juliet.'

George Bernard Shaw

Waste Not Want Not

'Every woman cares for hoarding lace, fur, and feathers, but Her Majesty goes further than this, and almost without exception, her wardrobe woman can produce the gown, bonnet or mantle she wore on any particular occasion.'

The Private Life of the Queen by One of Her Majesty's Servants, 1897

We are very amused!

Weddings

Mendelssohn's famous Wedding March was first played at a real wedding in 1858, when Queen Victoria's eldest daughter, Princess Victoria, married Crown Prince Frederick of Prussia.

Another tradition began at the same wedding when the newly married couple and the entire royal family appeared on the balcony at Buckingham Palace following the marriage service.

Weight

'Was weighed and to my horror weigh 8 stone 13!!'

Queen Victoria, *Diary*, 1838

'The best figure for a woman is fine and full with a fine bust.'

Prime Minister, Lord Melbourne, 1838, reassuring Queen Victoria about her weight

'When we were going down Craig-na-Ban – which is very steep and rough, Jane Churchill fell and could not get up again, (having got her

We are very amused!

feet caught in her dress) and Johnny Brown (who is our factotum and really the perfection of a servant for he thinks of everything) picked her up like *un scène de tragedie* and when she thanked him, he said, 'Your Ladyship is not so heavy as her Majesty!' which made us laugh much. I said, 'Am I grown heavier do you think?' 'Well I think you are,' was the plain-spoken reply. So I mean to be weighed as I always thought I was light.

Queen Victoria, *Journal,* 1849

Whisky

Queen Victoria was introduced to the delights of malt whisky by her Scottish servant, John Brown, a man well known for taking more of his native drink than was good for him.

One day John Brown announced he was taking the Queen on a drive and picnic into the Scottish countryside and that her lady-in-waiting would not be needed.

'You will be taking tea I expect?' inquired that lady anxiously.

'Well no, she don't much like tea – we tak oot biscuits and sperruts.'

Queen Victoria congratulated John Brown on producing the best cup of tea she had ever tasted.

'Well it should be, Ma'am,' he replied. 'I put a grand nip o' whisky in it.'

We are very amused!

'She (Victoria) drinks her claret strengthened, I should have thought spoiled, with whisky.'

Prime Minister William Gladstone, letter to Mrs Gladstone

The last thing Queen Victoria drank before she died was a glass of malt whisky.

Women's Rights

'We poor creatures are born for Man's pleasure and amusement.'

Queen Victoria

'I am most anxious to enlist everyone who can speak or write to join in checking this mad, wicked folly of "Women's Rights", with all its attendant horrors, on which her poor feeble sex is bent, forgetting every sense of womanly feeling and propriety. Lady —— ought to get a good *whipping*. It is a subject which makes the Queen so furious that she cannot contain herself. ... Woman would become the most hateful, heartless and disgusting of human beings were she to unsex herself, and where would be the protection which man was intended to give the weaker sex?'

Queen Victoria

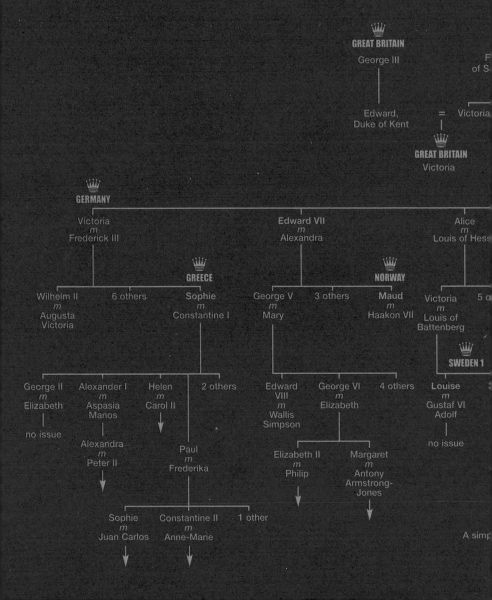

GREAT BRITAIN
George III

F
of S

Edward,
Duke of Kent
= Victoria

GREAT BRITAIN
Victoria

GERMANY
Victoria
m
Frederick III

Edward VII
m
Alexandra

Alice
m
Louis of Hess

GREECE
Sophie
m
Constantine I

NORWAY

Wilhelm II
m
Augusta
Victoria

6 others

George V
m
Mary

3 others

Maud
m
Haakon VII

Victoria
m
Louis of
Battenberg

5 o

SWEDEN 1

George II
m
Elizabeth

no issue

Alexander I
m
Aspasia
Manos

Alexandra
m
Peter II

Helen
m
Carol II

2 others

Edward
VIII
m
Wallis
Simpson

George VI
m
Elizabeth

4 others

Louise
m
Gustaf VI
Adolf

no issue

Paul
m
Frederika

Elizabeth II
m
Philip

Margaret
m
Antony
Armstrong-
Jones

Sophie
m
Juan Carlos

Constantine II
m
Anne-Marie

1 other

A simp